Forged by the Fire of Adversity:

Faith in Trying Times

By: Chelle Lynne

Copyright © 2009 by Chelle Lynne

Forged by the Fire of Adversity:
Faith in Trying Times
by Chelle Lynne

Printed in the United States of America

ISBN 978-1-61579-006-7

All rights reserved solely by the author. The author guarantees all contents are original and do not infringe upon the legal rights of any other person or work. No part of this book may be reproduced in any form without the permission of the author. The views expressed in this book are not necessarily those of the publisher.

Unless otherwise indicated, Bible quotations are taken from The King James Version of the Bible.

www.xulonpress.com

Thank you Lord for everything you have
done in my life.
I know I don't deserve such grace and mercy;
I am so grateful for your blessed gift of salvation
through your son Jesus Christ.

This book is dedicated to:

My children Zachary, Aidan and Alyssa (my angel), who have taught me so much about unconditional love.

Chaplain (Lt. Cdr.) Dwight Horn for being a constant source of inspiration and encouragement.

Our church family at Odenton Baptist Church for their love and support during the trying times.
and
Katrina for her prayers and unrelenting concern for my soul. She helped me to see that all I really need in my life is God, for he fulfills our every need, both known and unknown. Thank you for helping me to establish the one relationship that matters above all others, the one with my Lord and Savior.

INTRODUCTION

This book is the result of my spiritual journey over many years. However, in the past six years, I have learned more by opening my heart and my life to God than in all the years before.

Like many in this world of ours, I was a lost lamb who had wandered away from the shepherd. I had faith and I believed in God, but I had not done what he commands us to do. I had not called upon the name of the Lord and asked him to be my personal Savior. I had not established a personal relationship with Jesus and submitted to the will of God in my life. I was determined to set my own course for my life, and I vigorously mapped out my plans.

I was devoted to my career and willing to make any sacrifice to achieve the almighty promotion. My career came first, before everything else, even God and my own family. Soon I found the plans I had so meticulously shaped for myself did not always come together the way I intended. I always chalked it up to fate and coincidence, never even considering that there might be a plan more important than my own. After all, I knew what was best for me, right?

Well, God had a plan for me, and it didn't necessarily coincide with the plan I had mapped out for myself. When gentle reminders from God about who was really in control didn't work, he used a chain of traumatic emotional events to bring me back to the flock. You see, while I was as lost as I could be, yet thinking I was in control, God never gave up on me. He wanted me to find my way back home – back to my eternal home. Eventually, I did.

This book documents that journey – a journey of faith filled with joy and sorrow; laughter and tears; trials and blessings. My journey is not yet complete, but the Lord laid a burden on my heart to share what I have learned in my walk through difficult times. For through Him, anything is possible, even in the bleakest of circumstances. You just need to keep your faith.

If you are experiencing difficult times and reading this book, my wish for you is this:

> *Wherefore I desire that ye faint not at my tribulations for you, which is your glory. ... That he would grant you, according to the riches of his glory, to be strengthened with might by his Spirit in the inner man.*
> *Ephesians 3: 13-16*

Though this book is faith based because that is my anchor for the storms of life, even if you lack that faith, the concepts provided in this book can have application in your life. Whether you call it keeping a positive outlook, looking for the silver lining, the circle of life or paying it forward, the simple concept of reaching out to others in need applies across the board no matter what hardship you are facing.

I fill many roles in my life – daughter, sister, wife, mother, Soldier, and friend. None of these has been more rewarding than my role as a child of God. In letting go of everything I tried to control in the past, I have found more joy and peace in the knowledge that God has me in the palm of his hand. Walk with me on this journey of faith as I tell you my story.

TABLE OF CONTENTS

Chapter 1 – My Plan vs. God's Plan for Me 15

Chapter 2 – Analogies for Adversity 39

Chapter 3 – There Are No Coincidences..............49

Chapter 4 – Lean Not on Thy Self........................59

Chapter 5 – Our Promises and Our Instructions...73

Chapter 6 – Ask What, Not Why..........................87

Chapter 7 – Using Our Faith to Lift Up Others....93

Chapter 1

My Plan vs. God's Plan for Me

Trust in the Lord with all thine heart; and lean not unto thine own understanding.
Proverbs 3: 5

As a child, I always felt I had a special purpose in life. I was to do something important with my life. Back then, I wasn't sure what that meant for me; eventually I would figure it out, but I wasn't in a hurry. However, God knew his plans for me, and looking back on my life with my new spiritual view, I can see where he had been guiding me to the place he wanted me to be.

I wandered through much of my life trying to figure out where I fit in. I accomplished many things, both in school and once I started working, but I always felt there was something more just around the corner. With every accomplishment, I would strive for my next big goal, but none of these activities brought me any satisfaction. I was always looking for something more beyond what I could see. Something was missing from my life; but for the longest time, I couldn't figure out what that something was.

Growing up, I had a foundation of faith, but some of the church teachings just didn't make sense to me. I felt disconnected from what I was hearing, and I saw things that just didn't line up with my beliefs about what a church was supposed to be and do. When the church I grew up in refused to allow my grandmother to join because she had been divorced after 53 years in an abusive marriage, I made a decision to leave that denomination. Wasn't the church supposed to help bring people to God, not turn them away? Once I was out on my own, I set out on a journey of discovery. Surely there was a church denomination that fit with my beliefs about what a church should be, a place where I would feel comfortable; I just needed to find it.

Using my best research methods, I took a very methodical approach in my quest. I read many books. I attended many churches, sampling a variety of faith denominations the way one would sample different foods on a buffet. None of it satisfied my hunger. I was still left with a feeling that there was something more I just couldn't see. Little did I know, my worldly approach to this journey had spiritually blinded me. Instead of listening to what God was telling me in my heart and following the path he laid before me, I continued to navigate with my head by rationalizing every choice and decision based on personal desires. Eventually, I gave up on my spiritual journey and focused on building my life based on the worldly definition of success.

Being somewhat of a perfectionist, I wanted control of everything. I didn't like feeling as if I had no control over a situation. Part of my effort to control my life revolved around mapping out plans. I had a plan for my career and the things I wanted to accomplish. I pursued job promotions with reckless abandon, willing to make any sacrifice just to get ahead. I also had a plan for my personal life, mapping out my timeline for marriage and children. I thought I had the perfect timeline to do it all. I would be the superwoman who had everything - career and family - achieving success on both fronts. How foolish I was back then.

On several occasions, God used events to try and remind me that I was not the one in control, but I blindly continued on my ignorant path. When I thought I had timed my pregnancy perfectly with my personal and career plans, I had a miscarriage at the end of my first trimester. I continued to try and get pregnant again so I could keep my timeline in order, but struggled with infertility for more than a year. My plan was unraveling. How could that be? It had been such a perfect plan.

I pursued a different position at work that I had wanted so badly, but ended up being transferred to a position in a different unit. That wasn't the job I wanted. Once again, my plan was unraveling. It didn't matter that the position change helped me gain new skills and contacts that I otherwise would not have had. It wasn't what I wanted, and it wasn't in the plan that I had mapped out.

At the time, I couldn't figure out why things weren't working out the way I had intended. Looking back though, I see the error of my ways. I was following my plan, one I had mapped out without prayer, without reflection, and without a thought for what God wanted me to do with my life. I was focused on what the world deemed important – money, prestige, material possessions and social status – instead of the things that are important in the eyes of God. Even after my marriage failed and I was left to care for my son by myself, I still couldn't see that my priorities were completely skewed.

As I look back on my life now, I can see that God was still trying to bring me back from the vast emptiness of the world into His arms, despite my stubbornness. He convicted others to pray for me. He brought people around me to help guide me in the right direction, but in the end, the decision was still mine to make. The journey I would take over the next few years was not an easy one, but it was one I had to take because I had ignored the earlier gentle prods.

The first part of my journey home revolved around my introduction to a Christian man. Unbeknownst to me, one of my co-workers had a single friend he had known for several years, and he wanted to play matchmaker. After nearly a month of parading him past my office so he could see me, he arranged for all of us to go out for lunch. I was focused solely on my career and certainly had no intentions of pursuing any romances, especially after the disastrous end of my marriage. However, lunch out of the office was a welcome retreat from the stress of work, and it seemed harmless enough. That lunch was soon followed by several more lunches and long phone conversations about our lives, our dreams and our goals.

He treated me with the utmost respect. He was kind, gentle and witty. He certainly was much different than my abusive ex-husband. He listened to me. He talked to me as an equal. My battered and bruised self-esteem didn't know how to respond. I was leery, for fear of being hurt again. I had come to believe I didn't deserve this much attention or caring. Seven years of abuse had made me feel worthless, but he gently coaxed out my trust and my confidence until I started to blossom again.

Despite my resolve to stay away from any type of romance, I found myself falling in love with him. My feelings were completely unexpected, and I was caught off guard by the intensity of what I felt. In spite of every rationalization about why it was wrong to get involved with someone that soon after my divorce, it felt completely right. Everything about our relationship felt like I was right where I was supposed to be. Instead of fighting my feelings, I gave in to them and left myself wide open to whatever was going to happen.

Love blossomed, and soon we were talking about getting married. None of what was happening fit into any of the plans I had, because my plans didn't have anything in them about falling in love again. But I was quickly learning to roll with the changes. Little did I know, many more changes would follow close behind.

Shortly after our wedding, we found out I was pregnant. To say we were surprised would be an under statement, after all, I was on birth control. How could something like this happen? Apparently, changes in my prescription had allowed a window of opportunity we didn't anticipate. And God would use this opportunity to bring me the most incredible gift.

And whoso shall receive one such little child in my name receiveth me.
Matthew 18: 5

Nearly four months into my pregnancy, doctors became concerned about my platelet count, which had been dropping, and sent me for a detailed ultrasound to make sure my blood issue was not affecting the baby. I had experienced the same issue with my platelets during my first pregnancy and had no adverse effects, so I really wasn't concerned. Nothing I had experienced in life up to this point could have prepared me for what I was about to go through, not even 11 years of rigorous military training. I was about to be tested in ways I had never imagined.

During my ultrasound, the technician measured the baby's overall body size, head size, chest size, and the length of the large bones in the arms and legs. As the ultrasound progressed, I became concerned by the lack of information and the non-verbal signals the technician was showing. Something was wrong, but she wouldn't say anything. After the technician finished the measurements, she went to get the doctor. As I lay there waiting, I tried to calm my fears by telling myself that surely the technician would have said something if she had seen anything really serious. Wouldn't she?

The doctor finally came in after what seemed like a very long time and started taking some of his own measurements. He explained that the baby was measuring smaller than expected, especially in certain bone lengths, and there were some things they just couldn't see very well. Particularly troublesome were the femur lengths and a measurement on the back of the neck. The doctor explained that these markers could sometimes be an indication of Down Syndrome, and they wanted to do an amniocentesis to see if there was a genetic issue.

The amniocentesis was scheduled two weeks later. In the two weeks it would take for the results to come back, I scoured the Internet looking for all the information I could find on Down Syndrome. If I was going to have a baby with Down Syndrome, I was going to be prepared. When we received the results of the test, we were elated. The report said normal 46XY, a healthy baby boy. The good news was a relief, but that relief would be short lived.

With each monthly ultrasound, it seemed the doctors found something new about which to be concerned. Fuzzy pictures of the baby's spine, poor resolution on one kidney, and pictures that seemed to show a baby girl despite the amniocentesis results all worked together to make the doctors anxious. Yet for all of their concern, they couldn't tell us anything concrete. Each monthly ultrasound seemed to create more questions rather than provide any answers. It was unnerving. The monthly testing and lingering uncertainty began to wear on my husband and me, and after about three months, I came to a breaking point of sorts.

My husband was traveling at the time of my third scheduled appointment, so I went alone. The doctor discussed his inability to get a good, clear picture of the baby's spine beyond a certain point, but still provided no new information or concrete analysis of what the pictures really meant. I left with the same uncertainties as the previous two visits. That evening, the doctor called me at home to continue the discussion because he felt he had not effectively portrayed the seriousness of the situation with me in his office.

In a manner completely devoid of compassion, the doctor proceeded to tell me that my child would be born horribly disfigured, and I should consider aborting the pregnancy. His utter lack of tact and concern infuriated me. Abortion went against everything my husband and I believed and was not something we would consider. At this late stage in my pregnancy, even if we had considered it, abortion was not a legal option. The call greatly upset me. When my husband called 10 minutes after I had finished talking with the doctor, I was crying so hard that I couldn't even speak to him.

Once I calmed down, I thought about all the events of the past three months and made a decision. I would not worry about the doctors' conflicting information or lack of answers. I knew my baby was alive and developing because I could feel it every day, and I would not allow myself to become overly stressed. To many, I think it seemed as if I was extremely naive or in denial about the situation. I was neither.

The truth was that I realized I was not in control of the situation, but I could control how I reacted to it. Anger, fear and crying would not help the situation, but rather, make me feel worse and potentially harm my baby. I trusted that God had control of the situation, and in prayer, I put my pregnancy in His hands. God would give me the child I was meant to have, so I asked him to watch over me and my unborn child and left the rest up to Him. Through the sea of uncertainty, my faith gave me a sense of calm and peace for whatever lay ahead. It was a calm I would need in the days to come.

At 37 weeks of pregnancy, the doctors decided the time had come for delivery. The baby was still not growing at an appropriate rate, and another three weeks would not make much difference. Given the circumstances, the doctors felt there was more risk than benefit to both the baby and me if we waited. So I was scheduled for induction. The doctors did another amniocentesis to ensure that the baby's lungs were fully developed, and the test results gave them a green light to proceed.

Because my body had not started to prepare itself for delivery yet, the induction was a long process. Throughout the 36 hours, my husband and I had plenty of time to ponder what the delivery would bring. At this point, all we knew for sure was that the baby would be small, have shortened femur bones, and probably be ambiguous in the development of its sexual organs, meaning a boy that looked like a girl. Everything else remained to be seen once the baby was born. Mentally, we prepared for all of the possibilities we knew and mapped out our plans for dealing with them. Boy, were we in for a surprise.

At 12:45 a.m. on August 18, 1999, our special child came into the world. The flurry of activity in the delivery room was surreal; for despite all of the noise in the room, a cry was conspicuously absent. I was in a fog from the drugs, and couldn't really focus on anything. It felt like I was in a tunnel. Nearly a year would pass before my husband recounted the events as they unfolded.

The Neonatal Intensive Care Unit (NICU) team of doctors and nurses who had been standing by went to work. The head delivery nurse told my husband, "Your baby isn't breathing. Would you like to hold her now?" It seemed as if he was being given the chance to decide our child's fate. Our faith could only allow for one response. He replied, "Let the doctors do their job. If she's meant to live, she will. If she's not, she won't." Only God knew the plan for this child, and we would not interfere.

Several attempts at intubation failed. There was something blocking her airway, preventing her from taking a breath. Finally, the doctors were able to get a small-sized tube down her airway so she could breathe, and the frenetic pace in the room slowed just a bit. The doctor was finally able to examine her.

Forged by the Fire of Adversity

As expected, she was small, weighing only 4 lbs., 3ozs.; and the femur bones were much shorter than normal. However, two of our most basic premises based on testing prior to delivery had been destroyed. The first amniocentesis had said normal 46XY, yet this child appeared to be totally female. She was not an ambiguous male; she looked like a normal girl on the outside, minus a vaginal opening. There were no testes or remnants of a penis. On the birth certificate, the doctors put female for gender. The second amniocentesis right before delivery had said breathing should not be an issue because her lungs were fully developed, and she had been doing breathing movements in the womb. Yet for some reason, breathing had been a major issue after delivery.

These were not the only two ways technology had failed us. As the doctor examined our baby, he found other surprises. Despite monthly detailed ultrasounds using the best technology available, there were anomalies that couldn't be seen. She was missing both of her thumbs. Her hands were perfectly formed for the rest of the fingers, yet without thumbs. In six months of ultrasounds, no one had ever bothered to count fingers and toes. They merely assumed her thumbs were folded into her closed fists. She also had an imperforate anus, where her rectum had not developed to meet the descending intestine. She had no way to eliminate waste. These were the first obvious anomalies the doctors could find. In the days to come, there would be many other surprises.

As the doctors prepared to take our baby to the NICU, they placed her in an incubator and wheeled her to the side of my bed. Even through my post-delivery fog, I could clearly see the mission that was before me. I looked at my child lying behind the clear plastic incubator walls; and despite the turmoil of her delivery, she appeared pink and almost healthy and was looking directly at me. It seemed as if we were the only two in the room. Though I couldn't hold her, there was an instant connection as our gazes locked. At that moment, we were inexplicably linked, and I heard a voice speak to my heart.

"I am your gift. Trust and believe, for you will care for me," the voice said.

Then in an instant, she was gone, whisked off to the NICU at the adjacent Kosair Children's Hospital, and the fog returned. After that, everything between the delivery room and my hospital room was a blur as I dozed in and out.

Around 9:00 a.m., I woke up with a clear head and an aching heart. Was it real or had it been a dream? As I gazed at my husband sleeping in the chair next to my bed, I knew I had not been dreaming. The events as I vaguely remembered them were real and reminders of the previous 36 hours lingered even in my hospital room. There was no baby in the room with us. All of the doors in the ward had "It's a Boy" or "It's a Girl" written on the white board on the door, except for my room. Nurses avoided coming in unless they absolutely had to. The emptiness of the room and my arms was palpable. I didn't understand it. Our baby was alive, yet everyone else acted as if she was dead. It was a stark contrast of views that would follow us throughout her life.

That day started the steady stream of doctors who seemed to bring torpedoes aimed at our hearts with every visit. Each doctor brought more bad news. Soon, we were compiling a laundry list of defects that would make any parent shudder – imperforate anus, missing thumbs, shortened femurs, hypoplastic ribs, extremely small rib cage, misshapen collarbone, and only one functioning kidney. It was almost more than we could bear.

In between the doctors' visits, we would discuss the latest news, sharing our thoughts on whether any one or combination of these defects was insurmountable. Taken in small, bite-sized pieces, each individual anomaly appeared capable of alternate solutions or approaches – plenty of people had missing digits or limbs, many functioned with only one kidney, growth hormones could make bones grow, and surgery could fix the waste elimination issue. Then we were hit with the bombshell.

Dr. Wilkerson, the head neonatalogist, visited with news that gave us great pause. Further testing had shown that our child's left eye appeared to be missing or malformed, and the doctors weren't sure about the right eye. They had requested the ophthalmologist do a complete exam to make a determination and were waiting for her to arrive.

The news was devastating, and it led us into a series of deep discussions and prayer sessions that would help us build our approach to the situation. When the doctor left, my husband and I looked at each other, thinking our prior discussions had just been ripped to shreds. How could she overcome all of these other issues if she lacked sight? Would it be possible, or had we been naive in our assessments?

At that point, my husband told me he had reached his breaking point. "If the doctors come in with one more piece of bad news, I need to leave the room because I just can't take any more," he said. That one statement started a discussion that would lead to an epiphany for us.

Our discussion started as many do when something bad happens. It started with the questions. Why was this happening? What caused these anomalies? What were we going to do? Would we be able to provide the right care for our daughter? All of these questions seem completely reasonable to the average person given our situation. They would almost be expected. Yet our discussion could have gone in one of two very different directions. We could have remained focused on the present and the questions and allowed ourselves to spiral into a cycle of denial or self pity. Or we could focus on the future and what we needed to do to move forward from that moment in time. Using our faith which had carried us to that point, we chose the latter of the two options.

Initially, my husband and I looked internally for answers. We both wondered if there was something we had done that might have caused our daughter's birth defects. He was a veteran of Operation Desert Shield/Desert Storm and had been exposed to a nerve agent during the destruction of one of the chemical weapons caches. He was being followed in the Gulf War Syndrome study because of various symptoms such as memory loss and joint pain. Was that the cause? I had been processed to go to the Gulf Region and received all of my shots before my flight was later cancelled. Did the combination of our shots and the chemicals cause this? I thought I had done everything right during my pregnancy. I ate right, took my vitamins and exercised. But had I done something during my pregnancy that might have caused these issues? Did I somehow overdo it with the exercise? Then we looked externally for answers. We had several rooms in our home painted earlier in the year. Were the paint fumes responsible? Was there something in our water that caused it? It was a very dark time; and the initial questions, with the corresponding search for answers, was very painful for both of us.

Our faith carried us through that dark time. As we talked about our questions, our answers, our thoughts and our fears, we drew closer together instead of retreating apart. And we looked to God for the answers that we couldn't find ourselves. The answer He gave us was simple. There would be no answers to our questions, at least not now, and we would have to move on. We had a child who needed us, and we could not afford to waste our time and energy on futile searches that would yield nothing. We would need all the strength we had to deal with her situation.

As we talked, our answer became abundantly clear. God gave us the child we were meant to have. She was very special, and we would have to be equally special parents in order to care for her. This was not something we could do alone. Only through the grace and strength of God, would we be able to accomplish this task. Our child was counting on us, and failure was not an option.

At that moment, we crafted the approach that we would use to deal with our situation. While everyone else focused on the negative and what she didn't have, we would focus on the positive and what she did have. God had a plan for our little girl, or else she would not have survived in the delivery room. And we had to rely on the strength and wisdom of God to provide the love and care required to help her achieve that plan, whatever it was.

We named our daughter Alyssa Marie and set out on a parenting journey that would be challenging, to say the least, yet rewarding at the same time. We had the awesome opportunity to love and cherish this special little girl and watch the Lord work through her to reach so many people, including us. Through our trials, the Lord blessed us in so many ways.

Alyssa's life was filled with medical procedures from the very beginning. She had her first surgery when she was only 18 hours old to put in a colostomy so she could get rid of her waste. Like the trooper she was, she pulled through the surgery with flying colors. Eleven more surgeries would follow during the next two years, and each time, she would pull through with a strength and determination that could only come from God.

The first five months of Alyssa's life were a roller coaster for us. It seemed as if she was either doing really well or nearly dying, and you never knew which it would be day-to-day. We were juggling military duties and parenting duties, both at home and at the hospital, all while trying to keep life somewhat normal for our four-year-old son Zachary. Even if we were reeling, we wanted his life to remain calm and on schedule. My husband worked his normal hours while I went into work early. At lunchtime, I would drive the 50 miles to the hospital to consult with Alyssa's doctors and spend time rocking her for a couple of hours. Then I had to make the 50 mile drive home, pick Zachary up from the daycare across from his school, and head home to figure out what we would have for dinner. On Thursday evenings, Zachary had gymnastics lessons, so we did family night out for dinner afterward. At night, we would collapse into bed exhausted.

During this time, medical tests revealed little information about Alyssa's condition. Every genetic test the doctors did came back normal. Her array of anomalies fit no known syndrome in any book or database. The doctors were stumped. Alyssa was a one-of-a-kind child like they had never seen, and by-the-book procedures gave way to treatment by symptoms. Alyssa was writing her own book, and we all were learning to do things her way.

My husband and I had no formal medical training, so we watched and learned from the wonderful nurses who cared for our daughter. We learned how to work the ventilator and oxygen; how to breathe for her with an ambu bag; and the good, the bad and the ugly for the various numbers in a blood gas reading. These things became part of everyday life for us. Al and I made it clear from the beginning that we wanted to be hand-on parents. We wanted to monitor the ventilator settings and provided the necessary adjustments. We wanted to ambu bag her if she needed it. After all, we would be the ones caring for her when she came home. If she came home.

Even after three months of testing, doctors still couldn't figure out why Alyssa kept suddenly losing her airway. We didn't understand the severity of their concern, for we had never been present when it happened. Usually we would receive a phone call in the middle of the night from the neonatalogist on call, explaining that they had to reintubate her due to rising carbon dioxide levels in her blood gas or loss of her airway. But she was always resting comfortably afterward, and the doctors never seemed to be in a panic when they called; so we really didn't worry too much about it. That changed the day we witnessed it for ourselves.

We were visiting the hospital on a Saturday, and I was holding Alyssa on my lap in the rocking chair. Things on the ward were quiet, and Alyssa had had a good night. Suddenly, I watched my daughter turn several shades of purple as I was holding her, and her alarm started going off, indicating a falling oxygen level. Lynne, her nurse, calmly disconnected the ventilator and started hand-bagging Alyssa with the ambu bag until she turned pink again. Then she calmly reconnected the ventilator as if nothing had happened. Everything was back to normal, except with me. Though I hadn't shown a single flinch during Alyssa's little "blue spell," as the nurses called it, inside I was freaking out. I felt as if I had just watched my child die and then come back to life in a matter of minutes, all while I was holding her.

I had Lynne put her back in the crib for me while I stayed seated in the rocking chair. And then the tears came. "All I wanted to do was hold her," I sobbed.

Lynne came over and put her arm around my shoulders to comfort me. "It wasn't anything you did or didn't do. She just does that sometimes, even if no one touches her," she said. "Now you know why we call her the baby with attitude. She certainly makes it clear when she's not happy."

To the nurses, Alyssa's spell was just one of many they had seen, but for me, that day was life altering. It was the first time in three months that I allowed myself to even entertain the thought that Alyssa might not survive. That thought sent a chill through me that I couldn't shake, and I spent the rest of the day bursting into tears at the drop of a hat as I grappled with the thought of losing her. That night I prayed for the strength to deal with whatever happened to Alyssa. I asked God to help me be the caregiver I needed to be to help Alyssa achieve whatever plan he had for her. For I had seen His awesome power that day in the hospital; and I knew that it wasn't the machines, or any of us, that were keeping her alive. God was keeping her alive, and He had a reason for doing so.

The Lord answered my prayer. My connection with Alyssa became so strong over the months in the hospital that I could sense her every need. I had charted every trend in her care each day that she was alive in a journal, and I knew her better than any of the doctors or nurses. That word got around the NICU ward. Even the on call doctors would tell the nurses to call me at home if they had any questions about how to calm Alyssa or manage issues that might arise. These instincts that helped manage her care were not mine. I had no knowledge or formal training in nursing or medicine. I merely trusted the Lord and let Him guide me where I needed to go.

After nearly four months in the hospital, an MRI of Alyssa's chest finally revealed why she was having such difficulty breathing. Because of her small chest size, her heart was more in the center of her chest rather than off to the left as it should have been. Because of this, her aorta was laying on top of her airway. Every time she became agitated or upset, the aorta would swell with the rise in blood pressure and cut off her airway. Now that the doctors knew what was causing the problem, they had to figure out how to fix it.

The hospital's most prominent heart surgeon said a sling to hold the aorta up off her airway might provide the answer, but we would have to present her case to the Heart Board for review. Two presentations proved unsuccessful in persuading the surgeon to do the procedure. He didn't believe Alyssa would live even if he did the surgery. After several weeks, we went back to the board for a third and final time. The airway episodes were becoming more frequent, and we were running out of time. We showed data of her growth and stability, and the doctors and I made an impassioned plea, they in person and I through a letter.

"Alyssa is growing and thriving. She is trying, with every ounce of her being, to live. This procedure is her only chance," I wrote. "With the surgery, she may live or she may die; but without the surgery, she will surely die. It is not up to you to play God. Use your skill to help her, and let Him decide which way it goes."

The Heart Board accepted Alyssa for surgery, and the procedure was scheduled two weeks before Christmas. Everything was in the Lord's hands. The doctors and nurses in the NICU had doubts about whether Alyssa would survive the surgery, but my faith never wavered. I had prayed about it, and I knew in my heart that this surgery would mark a turning point for Alyssa. My faith proved true.

The surgeon opted to go through her ribs to reach the aorta, rather than cutting through her sternum, as they do for open heart surgery. This greatly decreased the risk during surgery. Alyssa not only survived, but bounced back quicker than anyone could have imagined. Within a week, she was out of the critical care room and back in her normal bed at the back of the ward.

The successful heart surgery allowed doctors to insert a tracheotomy for easier breathing, and Alyssa's progress from that point on was remarkable. She grew, she gained weight, and for the first time, she was able to spend time off the ventilator, breathing on her own. Her health improved every day, and her personality blossomed. She was still the baby with attitude and knew what she wanted, but coupled with that feistiness was a sweetness that poured out and touched everyone around her.

The roller coaster ride of ups and downs the first five months was over, and the next five months, while there were small bumps in the road, showed a sound upward trend of improvement. The doctors and nurses began to prepare for Alyssa's discharge from the hospital. We would need to have equipment and home nursing coverage in place to make the thought of discharge a reality.

On June 10, 2000, after ten months of waiting and wondering, Alyssa finally came home from the hospital. It was a day of joyful tears as she toured the NICU in her wagon to say goodbye to all of the doctors and nurses. These wonderful, caring people had become like family to us, and we would miss them. Cindy, one of the nurses who had been with Alyssa from the start and had become a dear friend, rode home in the van with us. She had offered to work some of Alyssa's home care on days she wasn't scheduled at the hospital to help with the transition. That small gesture provided great comfort to us as we took on the great responsibility of caring for Alyssa at home.

As we took our daughter home that day, we wondered what the coming days would bring. The doctors gave us no predictions. Alyssa had definitely surpassed their prediction at birth of living only three weeks. But with no definitive diagnosis, there was no prognosis for her either. Their advice was to continue her care as they had done in the hospital, managing her symptoms as they appeared. Let her tell us what she needed.

We chose to live each day with Alyssa to its fullest, counting each as a blessing from above. We would love her with all of our hearts and provide steadfast support so that she could achieve whatever was possible for her. In taking each day as it came, we trusted God would continue to give us the strength, knowledge and resources we needed to care for His precious gift.

Chapter 2

Forged by the Fire — Analogies for Adversity

There are several analogies frequently used to describe the adversity that Christians face in their lives. No matter which analogy one might prefer for explaining why our loving God allows adversity in our lives, one thing is clear. God has a distinct purpose behind everything that happens, good or bad. And if you trust in Him, He can use even the worst possible situations to bring about good.

Forging Metal

> *John answered, saying unto them all, I indeed baptize you with water; but one mightier than I cometh, the latchet of whose shoes I am not worthy to unloose: he shall baptize you with the Holy Ghost and with fire.*
>
> *Luke 3: 16*

Forged by the Fire of Adversity

The first analogy Christians often use for adversity ties into the title of this book. In metal work, forging is the process of using fire to superheat steel so that it can be shaped. People often think of sword making when they think of this process. The metal is heated in the fire and then pounded into the desired length and thickness. In this process of repeatedly heating, pounding and cooling, the steel becomes stronger while being molded into the shape desired by the sword maker.

In this analogy, the Lord is the sword maker and we are the steel. The fire is the adverse situations that we encounter in our lives. The heat of the situation makes us pliable so that God, our maker, can shape us and our lives. God uses adversity to mold us into the Christians He wants us to be.

Sometimes He uses the adversity to shift our focus or our priorities when they have turned away from Him. It is so easy for us to get distracted in our busy lives that our priorities become skewed. We get so caught up in work, school, home, our children's extracurricular activities, and our own socializing, we sometimes make everything else a higher priority than God. When this happens, our relationship with our Lord suffers as we pray less, leave the bible closed more often, and occasionally miss church services due to other scheduled events.

Adversity can be a stark reminder if we have forgotten that we need God in our lives. For at the first sign of trials, many people turn to prayer. When adversity brings us to our knees, prayer reaches out to the hand of God, and He helps us get back up again.

Sometimes the Lord uses difficult situations to bring us in contact with people who need to hear God's Word or see an example of Christian living. Too often when dealing with adversity, we think only of ourselves. Why me? How will this affect me? We get so wrapped up looking inside that we become blind to all else. That blindness causes missed opportunities for reaching out and touching the lives of others.

Sometimes our difficult situations may just be a reminder of His presence, an opportunity to watch God work in our lives. Too often we look at just the moment and miss the majesty of the Lord all around us. When we try to tackle our burdens with all that we as humans can muster, it is often not enough, and we fail. When we give our burden over to the Lord, we can watch him not only shoulder our load but provide bountiful blessings to us in the process. Our loving God doesn't want us to fail. He wants us to seek Him, but the choice is ours alone to make.

No matter how the Lord uses the negative things that come into our lives, one thing is certain. Just like the metal, we become stronger for the fires we go through. When we keep our eyes on the Lord, we gain wisdom and emerge out of the fire as stronger Christians, with a better understanding of God's presence in and will for our lives.

Purifying Gold

But he knoweth the way that I take: when he hath tried me, I shall come forth as gold.
Job 23: 10

Another analogy people frequently use when talking about how God uses adversity is the process of purifying gold. Coincidentally, this analogy also has fire in it as a critical element. Do you see a theme here?

In the process of refining gold, fire is used to purify the gold by melting it to a liquid form so that the impurities will rise to the top where they can be removed. The gold is then a better quality and produces jewelry with a greater shine and luster.

Even as Christians, sometimes we let impurities cloud our lives. When we say and do things that we shouldn't, we don't shine and reflect the light of the Lord. We lose our Christian luster, that which sets us apart from others and makes us a shining example.

The Lord tell us that all are to turn "…from darkness to light, and from Satan unto God, that they may receive forgiveness of sins, and inheritance among them which are sanctified by faith that is in me" (Acts 26: 18).

Lost souls all around us focus on the things of the world rather than the things of God. They seek money, possessions, prestige, all the while partaking in the evils Satan offers in this world – drugs, alcohol, sex, foul language. Even Christians, thinking they can resist Satan's lure, sometimes dabble in the things of the world, convinced that they cannot be consumed. They don't realize that once they open that door, they invite Satan in, and he will keep them from doing the Lord's work. They will not be a Christian example for others to follow. Remember, the Lord may test you, but He will never tempt you. That is Satan's work.

God uses the fire of adversity to purify us, burning away the impurities in our lives so we can shine as his light in a world of darkness. Adversity can rid us of vanity, pride, lust and the multitude of other things that will pull us toward the world. It provides an opportunity to refocus on the things that are really important.

Christian Pruning

I am the true vine, and my father is the husbandman. Every branch in me that beareth not fruit he taketh away: and every branch that beareth fruit, he purgeth it, that it may bring forth more fruit.

Now ye are clean through the word which I have spoken unto you. Abide in me, and I in you. As the branch cannot bear fruit of itself, except it abide in the vine; no more can ye, except ye abide in me.

I am the vine, ye are the branches: He that abideth in me, and I in him, the same bringeth forth much fruit: for without me ye can do nothing…

If ye abide in me, and my words abide in you, ye shall ask what ye will, and it shall be done unto you.

John 15: 1-5, 7

The final analogy frequently cited by Christians when examining the role of adversity in our lives is based on a gardening theme and is my personal favorite. This analogy uses the illustration of God as a gardener and equates adversity with the pruning of a plant.

There are four components in this verse – the Gardener, the Vine, the Branches, and the Purpose. Each one plays a critical role in the story.

The Gardener is God. Think of Him as the master landscaper. He is the one who has the landscaping plan and places each plant exactly where He wants it. He watches over the whole garden, faithfully and lovingly tending to each plant's every need. He also is the one who does the pruning. His pruning is not haphazard or random; it is a precise, methodical and purposeful process.

The Vine is Jesus and is the central part of the plant. The vine provides life for the branches by transporting fluid from the roots. A vine produces items just like itself – a grapevine produces grapes and apple trees produce apples. The vine of Jesus produces people who think and behave like Jesus. As we abide by Jesus and place him in the center of our lives, he increasingly is the source of our life, and our lives begin to look more and more like his.

The Branches are us. Branches are grafted to the vine. We are grafted to Jesus in a union formed by faith. Without the vine, the branches are nothing, so they must stay connected. As Christians, our way of staying connected to Jesus lies in the time-tested disciplines of prayer, reading the word of God and worship.

The Purpose is to bear fruit. An apple tree is not doing what it was intended to do if it does not produce apples. A rose bush is not doing what it should if it does not produce roses. They may be pretty, but they are not productive. Likewise, we are not doing what we are supposed to do if we are not bearing fruit for the Lord. Our purpose on Earth is to spread the word of God and grow, or produce, more Christians. If we are not fulfilling our purpose, pruning may be necessary.

The act of pruning a plant can be either simple or involved – it depends on the condition of the plant. But it must be done. Pruning a plant clips away the outgrowth and causes it to focus on its stem and roots to bring nourishment to the heart of the plant. The more wild and unattended a plant has grown, the greater the amount of pruning that is required. Extensive pruning can truly shock a plant, and it may look dead to the casual observer. But inside, the plant is drawing food and strength from the roots; and when the next growing season begins, the plant blooms larger and fuller than before. The plant is also stronger and better able to withstand the elements of nature – wind, heat, rain, drought, and pestilence.

As Christians, we need to be pruned. Sometimes the pruning is simple, and sometimes it shocks us. If left to our own devices, we branches will continue to grow outward and away from our vine, Jesus. We get drawn into the world and lose our focus, causing us to grow further away from God by branching out to seek the things the world offers. Our Christian pruning makes us focus on that which gives us eternal life and should be central in our lives – Jesus. With this focus, we grow bigger in our Christian endeavors, bearing more fruit for the Lord. We, like the plant, are stronger and better able to withstand the elements of the world that would draw us away from God. With pruning, we can grow more productive. Without pruning, we merely grow wild, branching out with no real direction or purpose in our lives.

Not the Same Person

> *Thus saith the Lord; Cursed be the man that trusteth in man, and maketh flesh his arm, and whose heart departeth from the Lord.*
>
> *For he shall be like the shrub in the desert, and shall not see when good cometh; but shall inhabit the parched places in the wilderness, in a salt land and not inhabited.*
>
> *Blessed is the man that trusteth in the Lord, and whose hope the Lord is.*
>
> *For he shall be as a tree planted by the waters, and that spreadeth out her roots by the river, and shall not see when heat cometh, but her leaf shall be green; and shall not be careful in the year of drought, neither shall cease from yielding fruit.*
>
> *Jeremiah 16: 5-8*

No matter which analogy one might use for adversity, the simple fact is we are never the same after going through it. Whether we are different in a positive way or a negative way is entirely up to us, for it depends on where our faith resides. Is our faith in ourselves, man; or is our faith in God? Because of free will, we get to choose.

I am not the same person I was six years ago before my daughter was born. I am vastly different in my priorities, my perspective and my passion for living. But I would not be this way had I not gone through those trials.

Taking the basic person that I was before, the Lord molded and shaped me into the person He wanted me to be. He burned off the impurities in my life that clouded my character. And he turned my focus back to the roots of my existence, that which gives me life. He did all this because I placed my faith in Him.

Where I once looked at my plan for my life, I now look for God's plan for my life. Where I once did things that were acceptable to the world, I now do only the things acceptable in God's eyes. Where I once sought to reap the fruits of my labor in the world, I now labor to bear the fruit of souls for God's eternal kingdom.

But I could have chosen differently. I could have placed my faith in man and been sorely disappointed. For many people had already written Alyssa off. I could have relied on my own knowledge and strength in caring for Alyssa, and surely I would have failed her. I could have blamed God for the situation we faced, turning away from him, and I would have been trapped in darkness, unable to see the light in Alyssa's life.

I saw a quote once that said, "If the Lord brings you to it, the Lord will bring you through it."

I could have chosen to do many things differently, and each one would have changed the course of the situation and the results. But I shudder to think of what those results might have been.

Chapter 3

There are No Coincidences

For it is God which worketh in you both to will and to do of His good pleasure.
Philippians 2: 13

As humans, we love to interpret events to find a meaning or causality to the way things work in our world. We are very fond of words such as coincidence, chance, fate, luck, karma and destiny when discussing life's events. None of these words can begin to describe the things that happen in our lives.

If you look in the Bible, you will not find the word coincidence anywhere. The word chance is used just six times, and it is generally man using the word in an attempt to interpret something that has happened, much like we do today.

The simple fact of the matter is there are no coincidences in life. There is a reason for everything that happens, even when we don't understand what it might be. Only God understands it all, for He is the only one who sees the entirety – what was, what is, and what will be. The rest of us are blind; and in our blindness, the best that we can do is to use our faith to trust God's design based on the promises that He made to us.

And we know that all things work together for good to them that love God, to them who are the called according to his purpose
Romans 8: 28

The concept of everything having a Godly purpose was once very foreign to me. I too used to interpret life's events from a worldly point of view. But as I watched God work through Alyssa, I came to understand this concept. And I truly believe there are no coincidences in life.

There were no coincidences in the people who were present in the hospital where Alyssa was born. Each of them had skills that would bring her into this world and ensure her survival. The Lord put us in a place surrounded by doctors with skill and compassion, nurses who truly loved our little girl and technology not available everywhere.

There were no coincidences in the nurses and therapists who came to work with Alyssa once she came home from the hospital and the results they produced. The Lord brought people who were highly skilled and capable of caring for Alyssa in an environment where there were no backups. They were compassionate in truly caring for both Alyssa and the rest of our family. In our eyes, they were family and we treated them as such.

In addition to caring for Alyssa, one nurse, Katrina, had a special calling, for the Lord convicted her to pray for and reach out to me. She took opportunities in our conversations to talk about her Christian beliefs, but more importantly, she was a true example of Christian living. I saw her reading her bible every day she worked in our home. She even sang hymns to Alyssa when she rocked her.

In our home surrounded by love, Alyssa blossomed and thrived. Her joyful personality developed as she grew and gained strength. She interacted with everyone, started smiling, and learned to communicate with us in her own way using certain sounds and switches. Her progress was amazing to watch, and her doctors were stunned as she greatly exceeded their limited expectations. Once again, she was teaching them that just maybe they didn't know or control everything.

There were no coincidences in our military move from Kentucky to the Washington, D.C. area. The Lord provided us with a beautiful home in an area with wonderfully supportive neighbors. The regional military hospital had teams of doctors who received Alyssa, learned her complicated case and provided very skilled medical care. Our case worker at the hospital, Linda, was instrumental in helping us schedule multiple appointments and obtain equipment required for Alyssa's home care. The inadequate public schools in our area led me to search for a private school in which to enroll Zachary. The

Lord provided a wonderful one when He led me to the Odenton Christian School just 10 minutes from our house.

In line with our move, it also was no coincidence that Katrina offered to come with us to ease the transition. She would help train the new nurses on Alyssa's schedule, likes and dislikes, and work some shifts on the schedule until the nursing agency could recruit a full team of nurses for us. She stayed with us for nearly two months, helping to get Alyssa settled in.

Of course during her stay, Katrina needed a ride to weekly church services, and she asked me to find a church for her to attend. Zachary's school was affiliated with Odenton Baptist Church, so the search for a church was already done. Since I was driving Katrina to church, I rationalized that it made more sense to stay for the service instead of driving home and coming back to pick her up. So Katrina and I began attending church together each week. Though small, these were the first steps I had taken in many years to move closer to God. For despite my having faith for all that time, I had really never acted on my faith. That was about to change.

As Katrina and I climbed in the car after attending our third service together, I felt the need to ask her some questions. Something I had experienced during the service triggered a yearning in me that was more powerful than anything I had experienced before.

"Katrina, I need to ask you a question, but you have to promise not to laugh," I said.

"Sure," she replied. "What is it?"

"Explain that part of the service they do at the end, called the invitation. We never did that at the church where I grew up," I said.

Katrina proceeded to explain what that part of the service was for. Then she said, "Why do you ask?"

Feeling a bit silly, I explained to her that during the invitation part of the service each week I would start to feel really strange. My knees would get weak, and I would feel flushed all over. Sometimes it would even be hard to breathe. And it was always at the same part of the service each week, when they did the invitation at the end. I always felt as if I needed to go to the front of the church.

By this time, Katrina, who had promised not to laugh, had a grin that spread across her entire face. "Michelle, that's the Holy Spirit working on you and telling you that you do need to go forward," she said. Did you ever read those verses I wrote down for you?"

Sheepishly, I admitted I had not. The paper was tucked inside the pocket of my bible carrier, where it had been since the day she gave it to me. I had always meant to read them but never seemed to get around to doing it.

Once we arrived at home, I fished out that piece of paper Katrina had given me so many months before, and we sat down to read the verses together. The yearning I had felt at church was still there, and I knew that God had something he wanted me to learn. So I listened and read with great intensity. And then we prayed. At that moment, I accepted the Lord as my Savior and began my personal relationship with

Him. It was August 12, 2001, a day that will remain forever etched in my mind as my day of salvation. The day I finally found my way home to my Father and secured my eternal resting place.

When Katrina and I finished, I went downstairs and confronted my husband in the kitchen. He was raised in a Christian home and had been saved since 1972. In our two years of marriage, he had never mentioned the things Katrina revealed to me.

"Why didn't you ever tell me about salvation? Why didn't you tell me about the things I needed to do?" I asked. "Were you just going to let me go to hell?"

He was amused at my indignation. "Sweetheart, I love you very much, and I absolutely want you to be in heaven with me," he said. "I may be many things, but one thing I'm not is stupid."

"What do you mean by that comment?" I asked.

"I have wanted you to know the love of Jesus like I do the whole time I've known you, but I knew if I tried to talk to you about it, you would think I was trying to change you," he said. "For that reason alone, you would have resisted no matter what."

I asked, "But if you wouldn't try, how was I going to know?"

"Knowing that I wouldn't be able to reach you, I did the best thing I could," he said. "I prayed for you, and I asked God to bring someone into your life that could reach you, someone you would listen to. And he did."

As strange as it sounded, I had to admit he was right. I had always been fiercely independent and a bit stubborn. I would have been too proud to admit that I was imperfect or lacking something in my life. I would have viewed any suggestions he made as personal assaults on my individuality, and I would have resisted even if I had known he was right.

And at this point, it really didn't matter. God had answered both his and Katrina's prayers. Through the Holy Spirit, he had convicted me to step out in faith and trust him with my life. It was time to follow His will instead of my own.

At the time, I knew my life would change based on my new relationship with God, but I truly couldn't know how much it would change.

In many respects, my new beginning marked a new beginning for our entire family. We became very involved at our church and attended weekly services on Wednesdays and Sundays. My husband took on the duties as head usher, while I worked in the nursery and taught Sunday school to the three-year-olds. Zachary attended Sunday school and Children's Church and had fun participating in Lighthouse Club on Wednesday evenings. Within our Odenton Baptist Church family, we were blessed with many wonderful friends and fellowship. In this environment, we all blossomed, even Alyssa.

Once again, as in Kentucky, the Lord surrounded us with nurses and therapists who were very skilled and compassionate. More than just employees, they became part of our family to form a net of love and care around Alyssa. They were a constant source of support.

In this loving, supportive environment, Alyssa progressed even more than before. She began to sit up and watch videos on television. "Bear in the Big Blue House" and "Clifford" were her favorites. In line with her father's hobbies, she also enjoyed watching football. She learned to take a bottle and eat with her mouth to supplement her tube feedings, a very difficult feat when dependent on a ventilator. She even learned to blow kisses, and would frequently use that talent to flirt with her male caregivers.

Each and every piece of progress was a blessing that we cherished. Her doctors were stunned and expressed disbelief. Based on their best medical knowledge, there was no way she could be doing the things she was doing. Their analysis was based strictly on medical technology, so it was easy to see why they were amazed. They just didn't get it. We were amazed for a different reason. We recognized her abilities and progress came from God. There was no earthly explanation, and our amazement stemmed from watching Him work in her life every day.

Also during this time, we found out I was pregnant again. We had been hesitant to have another child after our experience with Alyssa's birth, but genetic testing revealed nothing to suggest a possible reoccurrence of her anomalies. Doctors monitored my pregnancy closely, and we trusted that God would once again give us the child we were meant to have. In July 2002, we welcomed our son Aidan into our family. He brought new joy to our lives, and our family routine added bottle feedings and diaper changes to the mix.

I remain steadfast in my belief that there were no coincidences in anything that happened during that three year period. Everything that happened had a purpose, and it was all part of God's plan for our lives. We couldn't necessarily see it as it was happening, but looking back afterward, we could see the path He had paved for us. Each event along the journey brought all of us closer to God, all because we kept our faith in Him. As we were faithful to Him, He faithfully blessed us in ways we could have never anticipated.

Yet even as we counted our blessings, we became comfortable in our daily lives. Each of us settled into a routine consisting of some combination of commuting, work, school, daycare, church, social activities and medical appointments. Our routines made it easy to think that nothing would change. The predictability was comforting, and in essence, we were lulled into a false sense of security. Focused on God's precious gift of each day, we no longer anticipated tomorrow. Little did we know, the greatest test of our faith was still before us.

Chapter 4

Lean Not On Thy Self

Trust in the Lord with all thine heart; and lean not unto thine own understanding.
Proverbs 3: 5

It was January 10, 2003. We had just finished celebrating a quiet, yet busy, holiday season. We stayed close to home and celebrated with just ourselves and the nurses. It would have been too difficult to travel the five hours to Ohio or nine hours to Michigan to visit with our families.

The Christmas decorations were packed away, and it was time to return to our normal schedules. My husband and I were back to our usual hours at work, and Zachary had returned to school following the holiday break. We were back into our comfortable routines.

The knock on our bedroom door came at 4:20 a.m. that morning. It was a knock that would shatter our routines forever.

The nurse said he needed my help, so I threw on my robe and stumbled across the hall into Alyssa's room. I was used to helping when she threw them a curveball; after all, I knew her better than anyone else. I was not prepared for what I saw that morning.

Her alarms were going off, and the nurse was doing CPR on her. He said she had been warm earlier that morning, and her sensors had been acting funny. Right before he came to get me, her monitor had gone off indicating a lack of pulse. He checked the sensors and then manually checked her for a pulse. When he found none, he started CPR and then had come to get me.

My instincts immediately kicked in, and I did all the things I knew from past episodes. As he performed CPR, I tried suctioning out her tracheotomy. No mucus came out, but it almost felt as if I was hitting something with the catheter. There wasn't time to change her trach. As he did chest compressions, I used the ambu bag to push air into her lungs.

I grabbed the phone and dialed 911. When the operator answered, I told them we needed and ambulance, giving them a brief description of what was happening. We had given our local fire house a heads up about Alyssa's situation when we moved into the neighborhood, so they sort of knew what to expect if they were called to our house. The operator asked if I wanted to remain on the line, but I told her I needed both of my hands to help the nurse. We were moving rapidly in our actions, but it felt as if we were in slow motion.

As we feverishly worked on her, my eyes took in the sights before me. Her usual pink color had been replaced by a dull grey. Fluid was coming from her nose with each ventilated breath, and there was blood in her colostomy bag. She was unresponsive in a way I had never seen before. Though my body wouldn't stop what it was doing, deep in my heart I just knew she was gone.

The rescue workers arrived, and they took over from us. We carried her out to the ambulance and placed her in the back. Our nurse climbed inside with the workers to assist. The crew told me to change clothes, and I could ride in the front seat to the hospital. As I headed into the house, it finally dawned on me that I had been outside in my robe and bare feet. I hadn't even noticed the cold. My focus was elsewhere.

I raced upstairs and changed into the first clothes I could find. Then I grabbed a pair of shoes and headed for the door. My husband met me at the front door with a travel mug of hot coffee.

"Here, you're going to need this," he said. "I'll get Aidan to daycare and Zach to school and meet you at the hospital."

I looked at him for what seemed like a lifetime, wanting him to be able to come with me, yet knowing he couldn't.

"How am I going to know what to do?"

"Trust your instincts," he said. You'll know what to do."

As I rode to the hospital in the ambulance, I tried to listen to what was going on in the back. Everything about the ride seemed so surreal. The hospital was only about 10 minutes from the house, but it felt like we were driving much longer. The driver took great care not to jostle the crew working on Alyssa in the back as he drove.

When we reached the hospital, the emergency room crew took over. I watched from the side as they continued CPR and administered various drugs. The scene was playing out just as I had imagined it would. As Alyssa's primary caregiver, I had always figured I would be there by myself when the final decisions were made. Yet even though I had spent three years preparing myself for this day, all I could think at the time was, "I'm not ready for this. I'm not ready to let her go." The reality is, whether death comes suddenly or gradually, we are never ready to let go of the ones we love.

After several rounds of drugs, CPR and then checking for a pulse, I moved up to the side of table. I held Alyssa's hand and smoothed her hair back. I asked our nurse whether she had responded at all in the ambulance. He said she did not. My husband was right; I knew what I had to do.

"That's enough," I said to the emergency room crew. "Just stop. Stop."

As the monitor went into its final flat line, I leaned down and kissed my baby girl.

"I'm sorry, baby. I couldn't save you this time," I whispered. "It's time for you to finally rest. Your fight is over."

Not knowing what to say, the hospital staff left the nurse and me alone in the room with Alyssa. I was numb yet still rational in acknowledging that I needed to make several phone calls. First I called home to tell my husband. We agreed he shouldn't say anything to Zachary just yet. Together we would formulate a plan for telling him later that day when we picked him up from school. Next I had to call the nursing agency so they could call off the nurse due to show up at 7:00 a.m. for her shift. I then called my boss at home and asked him to contact our unit chaplain for me. Finally, I called my mother in Ohio to tell her the news.

After the flurry of phone calls, I was drained. The nurse and I sat together and held Alyssa, stroking her hair and reminiscing about her short life and waiting for Al to show up. He was devastated and seemed to be in shock same as me. Nothing I said could console him. So we just sat together in our grief and waited. I glanced across the room at Alyssa's ventilator, thinking it odd that it was so far away. I had to fight an overwhelming feeling of needing to reattach it to her. It felt strange to hold her with no tubes attached. I had never been able to do that, and I didn't want to. The rational calm that had been with me initially was gone, replaced by a panicked need to turn back the clock.

When Al finally arrived, he was accompanied by Melanie, another one of our nurses. The agency had not been able to reach her to tell her not to come to work. When she arrived at the house for her shift, Al had to break the news to her.

The chaplain arrived, bringing with him my dear friend Cecily from work. That morning, the Lord surrounded us with a loving web of Christian friends who prayed with us, cried with us, and laughed with us. It was the first of many webs that would support us in the months that followed.

Back at home, the silence in the house was deafening. No hum from the machines. No beeps from the monitors. No whoosh of air through the ventilator tubes. There was only stone cold silence that cut through the air like a knife.

I found myself furiously scrubbing the carpet next to Alyssa's bed to get rid of the stains before Zachary came home from school. I had to keep busy. Then I had to scrub myself.

Death has a smell, and it was all over me. In the flurry of activity, I hadn't noticed it, but it hit me once we were home. Even after showering, I couldn't seem to get rid of the sickly sweet smell that lingered on me. I scrubbed and scrubbed, but the smell stayed with me for the rest of the day, a reminder of all that had transpired. As if I needed one.

As we made funeral plans in the next few days, I was numb to everything around me. Aidan's routine of feedings, diaper changes, naps and baths were the only things that kept me moving, almost as a robot. I was merely going through the motions. In a way, I felt dead, but the pain in my heart reminded me that I was very much alive. At times, my heart ached so much that I could barely catch my breath. But I had to keep moving. Zachary and Aidan needed their mom.

Both of our families came in for the viewings and the funeral service. It had been nearly four years since we were all together for our wedding reception. It was a bittersweet time.

My husband's family had not seen Alyssa since she was five months old. At the funeral home, they heard story after story about Alyssa's sweet spirit and spunky personality. I couldn't help but hope they realized everything they had missed by staying away for so long. They had lost their opportunity to get to know our amazing little girl.

My parents had recently visited in the summer. They both cherished the time they had spent with Alyssa, capturing on film and bragging about the special smiles they had received. My mother couldn't seem to stop crying, continuing a pattern she had started when Alyssa was born. She never could see any of the positive things. Instead she would say, "Oh, poor baby," convinced that Alyssa had suffered each and every day of her short three-year life.

Those of us who were with Alyssa on a daily basis knew otherwise. Her life was rich, not poor. In three short years, she had experienced more love and friendship than many people see in a lifetime. And in that time, she had impacted the lives of so many people.

Alyssa's funeral was a testimony to her life, upbeat and full of hope. Al and I wanted everyone present to know that we knew where our little girl was and that we would see her again when it was our turn to go home to our Father's house. It was important to us that they saw the hope that comes from our salvation, even if they didn't individually believe it.

As a baby Christian, having been saved for just more than a year, I felt as if my fellow Christians were watching me closely to see how I handled the situation. Would my faith falter or stand strong?

When adversity enters our lives, it can set up a tug of war between what we as Christians believe and what we as humans feel. It is a tug of war between our faith and our frailty. I experienced this battle firsthand. As a Christian, I knew my daughter was in heaven. I also knew that because I was saved, I would see her again when I died. But as a human, I hurt. My heart literally ached. As a parent, I wanted my child back. To the world, I showed a strong, faithful front. When alone, I cried the tears of pain and sadness from my loss.

Be sober, be vigilant; because your adversary the devil, as a roaring lion, walketh about, seeking whom he may devour.
1 Peter 5: 8

It is in this tug of war that the Devil finds his playground. Our salvation makes our spiritual side off limits to Satan. Our soul belongs to our Lord and Savior, and we are filled with the Holy Spirit. We are children of God. With no chance of capturing our souls, Satan's only recourse is to try to keep us from winning other souls for God. So he attacks the weakest part of us, our human nature. He attacks our physical body, our thoughts and our emotions. If he can turn our focus from our spiritual side toward the physical, mental or emotional side of us, he can keep us from growing as Christians and working in the world for God. Illness, injury, negative thoughts, inappropriate thoughts, depression and anxiety are just some of the ways the devil tries to turn our focus from God. Our faith is what keeps us strong against these attacks. I learned my lesson on this the hard way.

My husband and I went back to work exactly one week after Alyssa's funeral. Operations in Iraq were getting ready to kick off, and as military officers, we had a job to do. It was easy to immerse ourselves into work and not deal with our feelings. Ignoring the pain became our pattern, but this type of strategy doesn't work well for long.

About five months after Alyssa's passing, I went to school for three months in another state. All of a sudden I found myself away from my family and in an environment where I had much more time on my hands. Everything I had repressed and ignored for the past five months came to the surface with a vengeance. I could no longer bury the pain. I had to deal with it. And this is where I stumbled in my Christian walk.

As I tried to deal with the sudden rush of repressed emotions, I took my eyes off God and focused on my human feelings. By focusing on the human rather than the spiritual side of me, I was trying to deal with the situation by myself with only the strength I possessed. It was not enough, and without realizing it, I opened the door for the devil to attack me.

Each night, I would relive the morning that Alyssa died in my dreams, experiencing the sights, smells and emotions all over again. I would wake up in the morning as tired as I had been the night before. Soon my emotions were spinning out of control, and deep depression set in. I could barely function. I began to turn to alcohol to deaden my senses, hoping I wouldn't feel the pain anymore.

Yet in the midst of this downward spiral, a small voice spoke to me repeatedly saying, "You are not alone. Let God help you."

One day after classes, I went to the Christian bookstore at the mall. Surely I could find something there to lift my spirits. As I wandered the aisles, I let the Lord lead me to the spiritual nourishment He felt I needed. I purchased two things that day, a book called *Comfort for Christians* and the music CD Worship by Michael W. Smith.

When I returned to my room, I immediately put the music on and settled in to read my new book. The book was small, so I figured it would be a quick read. I was right. Start to finish, I think it took me only 40 minutes to go through the entire book, but in that time a transformation happened. As I read the book and listened to the music, so much of what I read and heard spoke directly to my heart. By the time I finished the book, I was in tears. I finally realized the error of my ways for the past five months. All this time, I had been trying to deal with my situation and my pain alone, when all I really needed to do was turn it over to God.

As I finished, I got down on my knees, and I prayed and cried harder than I ever had before, pouring out everything I had been holding in.

"I can't do this by myself anymore, Lord," I prayed. "I am weak, and only your strength will get me back on track in my Christian walk with you. I'm turning my burden over to you, Lord. Here it is."

As I kneeled there praying, I literally felt a weight lifting off my shoulders. I had turned my burden over to the Lord, and He had taken it from me. For the first time in my life, I understood the concept of peace that passes understanding. I was calm. I was unafraid. I was renewed. I was joyful. And I felt a need to share what I had just experienced. I called my husband first and then told a fellow student from my bible study group. I was practically giddy with happiness as I recounted for them what I had experienced that night. In the two years since my salvation, I had read the bible and prayed, but this was my "ah-ha" moment, the moment that I truly got it. I understood what it meant to stand solely on faith, nothing else, and trust God.

This book is a product from that night as well. So many people had told us through the years that we handled the situation with Alyssa in a manner very different from other parents of special needs children they encountered. They encouraged us to share our approach with others. We appreciated their kind words, but never really thought of following up on them. We knew the foundation of our unique approach was our faith, but we weren't sure other people would be receptive to that message.

For months after Alyssa's death, I felt the Lord tugging at my heart. In many respects, taking care of Alyssa had been my mission in life. I was fully dedicated to providing the best possible care and helping her to achieve whatever God intended for her. Once she was gone, I felt lost, and I had prayed to God for guidance on what my new mission would be. And he answered. For months, he laid a burden on my heart to continue the work he had started with Alyssa, to continue impacting other lives. He planted the seed of the idea for a book with me and continued tugging at my heart. All the while, I put Him off. It's too soon. I'm not ready. Why would God want to use me to spread a message? In essence, I ignored God's calling, and made excuses for why I wasn't doing what He asked me to do. And for a while, He let me get away with it. That changed the night I went to Him on bended knee.

As I tearfully prayed that night, turning my burdens over to him, I also acknowledged that I had been ignoring His calling.

"I know you've been tugging at my heart Lord to write a book, and I haven't done anything with it," I prayed. "I don't understand. Why me? I'm just a baby Christian. I can think of so many other people who are better Christians than I am. Why do you want to use me?"

I heard the Lord answer my questions. "Because I chose you," He said. "And I've given you what you need to do the job. You just need to go do it."

At that moment, I pledged to stop the excuses and follow God's calling. And I started writing. It may be my story, but the words are not mine. For each time I sat down to type, I prayed for the Lord to guide my hands in spreading a message, His message, so that it would impact the lives of others. And He did.

Chapter 5

Our Promises and Our Instructions

When faced with difficult times, we often look for ways to get out of the situation or to minimize the pain. In our human nature, we seek out help from doctors, therapists, mechanics, repairmen, financial advisors, counselors and pastors. In reality, we need to look no further than the Bible to find two things — first, promises the Lord makes to us, his children, and second, our instructions for dealing with difficulty. It is here we find our words of encouragement when we are discouraged.

Our Promises

There will be difficult times

These things I have spoken unto you, that in me ye might have peace. In the world ye shall

have tribulation; but be of good cheer; I have overcome the world.
John 16: 33

The first promise we have from God is that we will have tribulations in this world. He is very upfront and matter-of-fact in telling us life will not always be a bed of roses. There will be thorns along the way. Why, then, do we act surprised when these tribulations happen? We shouldn't be. Man opened the door to all the bad in the world with the very first sin in the Garden of Eden. Mankind has been mostly on a general downward trend ever since.

Paul discussed his adversity, his "thorn," in the book of 2 Corinthians, chapter 12. But he did not complain about his situation, rather he rejoiced in it. "Therefore, I take pleasure in infirmities, in reproaches, in necessities, in persecutions, in distresses for Christ's sake: for when I am weak, then am I strong." (2 Cor 12:10)

Jesus overcame and can overcome anything in the world. This is the very reason that Jesus told us to be of "good cheer." For when we rely on the Lord, He gives us the strength to withstand anything the world throws at us.

I will never leave you

"...For he hath said, I will never leave thee or forsake thee."
Hebrews 13:5

The Lord's statement that he would never leave us or forsake us is a promise we can count on at all times. He recognizes us as his children and is there for us always, even when we don't acknowledge his presence. Any separation we have from God is of our own doing.

When we focus on ourselves, the world, and anything else that pulls our eyes off of God, we place other things in our life as our priority. We push God to the background while our attention is focused elsewhere.

But God doesn't go away. He never gives up on us. Even when we push Him away, He remains ever present, waiting for us to return.

In times of tribulation, God is there for us. As we focus on the troubles at hand, at times we allow ourselves to feel as though the Lord has abandoned us. We foolishly listen to others when they say that a loving God would not allow these bad things to happen. We postulate that maybe God has given up on us. Nothing could be further from the truth.

God never gives up on us. Remember, God created us in his image, but man brought sin into the world and separated himself from God. We opened the door for all the evil in the world that results in our trials. We gave the Devil his playground, and he takes full advantage of it. God allows these things to happen as a reminder to us of our sinful nature. Yet through it all, he reminds us that He gave us a way to change the course we charted. He gave us His Son as our Savior – our way to walk with God again. All we have to do is accept that gift. Through Jesus, we are no longer separated from God.

In our trials, He waits for us to call on Him for refuge from the storm. All we have to do is ask. If the Lord brings you to it, the Lord will bring you through it; but you have to rely on him instead of trying to do it by yourself.

I never once blamed God for Alyssa's condition, and I never felt he had abandoned us. From the very beginning, I knew Alyssa was a tremendous gift from Him, and I felt His presence and His guiding hand at every turn during our three years with her. By keeping my faith during that time, I learned more about God and more about myself than I could have ever imagined I would.

We did not have the background, experience or knowledge to deal with Alyssa's medical issues, but I trusted God would help us navigate the course he set out for us. In turn, he surrounded us with wonderful, caring people who educated and trained us. I relied on Him to infuse me with the instincts I would need to provide Alyssa the proper care, and he did. Through my faith, I was so connected with Alyssa that I could anticipate her needs before she even expressed them. This allowed me to be both her caregiver and advocate. In short, we absolutely trusted God, and He in turn, provided everything we needed for the situation.

I will care for you

"Are not five sparrows sold for two farthings, and not one of them is forgotten before God? But even the very hairs of your head are all numbered. Fear not therefore: ye are of more value than many sparrows."
Luke 12: 6-7

Often we think we know ourselves and others close to us better than anyone else. We forget that God knows each and every one of us best. He knew us even before we came into being. As the scripture says, he even knows the very number of hairs on our head.

This scripture from Luke reminds us that God will care for us no matter how bleak the situation. Just as He provides for the smallest of creatures during harsh winters, He provides for us because we are of greater value. After all, we were created in His image. And we are charged with the most important mission — spreading His word to the ends of the earth so that all will know the truth.

Just as God knows us, He knows our every need before we can even utter them. He can and will meet those needs if we only let Him. Too often we try to do everything by ourselves with only our human abilities, and then we wonder why it doesn't work.

I will give you strength

> *"But they that wait upon the Lord shall renew their strength; they shall mount up with wings as eagles; they shall run, and not be weary; and they shall walk and not faint."*
> *Isaiah 40:31*

In times of trouble, our strength comes from the Lord. "It is God that girdeth me with strength, and maketh my way perfect." (Ps 18: 32) If we try to rely merely on what we have inside ourselves, it will be insufficient for navigating the situation the way God wants us to.

That is why we are instructed to draw our strength from the Lord every day, not just on bad days. God gives us strength for the day. Our problems come when we try to use the strength God gave us for today to tackle anticipated problems from tomorrow or even next week.

We need to trust that God gives us what we need to tackle the things we will face today and not worry about tomorrow. For tomorrow, God will give us what we need then. The book of Matthew tells us, "Take therefore no thought for the morrow; for the morrow shall take thought for the things of itself. Sufficient unto the day is the evil thereof." (Matt 6:34) Trusting for today and not worrying about tomorrow takes faith.

This trust goes back to the other promises we have that God will always be with us and will take care of us. This means he will provide for our every need.

Take stock in that promise and believe that you have what you need from God to tackle the challenges of today. New challenges will come tomorrow and next week, but God will give you what you need then as well.

Take each day as it comes and use the strength the Lord gives you to follow the path set before you. If you feel you will falter, pray for God to bolster your strength. He will deliver the strength you need to fly like an eagle through any challenge you face. He will give you the strength you need to run the race and not get tired, to walk the walk of faith without worry.

The simplest explanation of this promise is found in one statement from the book of Philippians, "I can do all things through Christ which strengtheneth me." (Phil 4:13)

Our Instructions

Thanks in making your requests

> *"Be careful (anxious) for nothing; but in every thing by prayer and supplication with thanksgiving let your requests be made known unto God."*
>
> *Phil 4: 6*

Too often we are quick to make our requests to God, but we forget to give thanks for the things we have received. Our blessings in life are abundant, and we often take them for granted.

In the Bible, our instructions are clear. We are to both give thanks, and make our requests known. Of note, the passage also mentions that we shouldn't be "careful" or anxious. In essence, the Lord expects us to be faithful in trusting Him, by giving thanks for the blessings he bestows so abundantly upon us and placing our requests before him.

Many people interpret this passage as meaning we should be thankful for the material things we have in life and letting Him know what else we want. This couldn't be further from the truth. We are expected to be thankful for all of the blessings in life that we receive but don't deserve – the simple and the complex. Each morning before I get out of bed, I thank God for giving me another day on this earth to serve him.

Our thanks can be for the simple things in life such as the sunshine in the sky and the birds that sing in the trees. Our thanks can be for the individual blessings we receive such as our parents, our spouse, or our children. We should give thanks for the provisions the Lord provides for us in accordance with His promise to care for us just like He cares for the sparrows. We have so much to be thankful for, the list is endless.

In these instructions, it is clear that the thanks should come before the requests. Many times we follow the reverse order, or forget to give thanks at all. It is easy when we focus on the world to take our blessings for granted or somehow come to believe we are entitled to the things we receive. This type of attitude is avoided when we remain humbly thankful for all that God gives us and make our requests with Him in mind.

Often our requests come in the form of material things we want or help in dealing with situations that arise in life. Too often, the requests we place before God are focused on our wishes and desires, which is the exact opposite of what God commands. Our requests ought to retain a heavenly rather than worldly focus and be made within the context of God's will in our life. In everything we ask, we should be seeking to serve the Lord and follow the path He wants us to follow.

Pray always

"Pray without ceasing."

(1 Thess 5:17)

Prayer is a critical component of our relationship with God, not just in times of trouble, but all the time. It provides the opportunity for talking to and drawing nearer to our heavenly Father in our daily walk of faith. Without a prayer relationship, why should God answer the call just because there is something we want from Him?

Prayer is the way to give thanks for blessings bestowed upon us and to seek to know God's designs for our lives. In our desire to seek God's will, everything in our lives should be laid before the Lord in prayer – every decision, every choice, every hardship, every blessing, and everyday life.

A solid prayer life establishes God's prominence in our lives. If we don't acknowledge God in our daily lives, why should he acknowledge us when we ask for His help? Our personal relationship with our Lord and Savior is not one of convenience. It's one of necessity. Through Christ, God gave us the free gift of salvation. But if you don't accept Christ as your personal Savior, the gift of eternal life in Heaven remains out of reach.

Prayer without ceasing acknowledges that God is the central focus of our lives and that we seek to serve His will for us. It acknowledges that the work we do here is not for the here and now, but rather, for the ever after of our life in eternity.

Give me your troubles

> *"Come unto me, all ye that labour and are heavy laden, and I will give you rest."*
> *Matt 11:28*

When we are faced with heavy burdens in life, God tells us to turn those burdens over to Him. He will take the load from us. Often pride and stubbornness keep us from doing just that.

I know this is the approach I used to take with problems. My personal pride wouldn't let me ask for help from anyone. I could deal with it all on my own. Stubbornly I would struggle along, doing my best to deal with life's curve balls, while trying to maintain an appearance of composure and calm. I wasn't very good at it, of course.

God doesn't like to see us struggle. He wants to make things easier for us. That's why he tells us to turn our difficulties over to him. "Casting all your care upon him; for he careth for you." (1 Pet 5:7) By turning over our burdens, He provides us peace of mind and heart.

I had often heard the phrase "peace that passes understanding," but I had a hard time really understanding the concept. "And the peace of God, which passeth all understanding, shall keep your hearts and minds through Jesus Christ." (Phil 4:7) That all changed when I reached my breaking point after Alyssa's death.

After trying to deal with everything I was thinking and feeling by myself, and failing miserably, I reached a point where I acknowledged I couldn't continue that way anymore. I was so miserable; yet when I turned everything over to the Lord, I instantly felt a peace I had never felt before. It was a peace that defied the situation I was in, a peace that seemed illogical to those around me. To me, it made perfect sense. I was no longer relying on myself. I was relying on God, and He provided the very things he promised.

You will be better for it

"...we glory in tribulations also: knowing that tribulation worketh patience; and patience, experience; and experience, hope; and hope maketh not ashamed; because the love of God is shed abroad in our hearts..."
Romans 5: 3-5

As difficult as it is to go through life's trials, it is absolutely amazing to see how much you change from the experience. When you emerge into the light from a period of darkness, you find that you are stronger, better grounded, and in many respects, you are a different person than you were before the experience.

Adversity can do one of two things to a person. It can tear them down or build them up, and the end result is largely dependent on from where the person draws their strength. People who rely solely on their own strength tend not to weather adversity as well as those who draw their strength from their faith in God and the love of others around them.

I am a vastly different person now than I was before Alyssa was born. Had someone asked me if I would be able to do some of the things I had to do with Alyssa before that experience, I would have answered with a resounding no. Sometimes we just don't know what we are capable of until we are put to the test. We do what we have to do, especially when it comes to the ones we love. I relied on the strength of God to help me in my mission of caring for Alyssa. I knew I couldn't do it by myself, so I took His lead. His hand guided mine in every procedure and every step of her care. I often look back at that period in joyful wonder at what He was able to accomplish through her despite everyone's perceptions of her limitations.

To everyone looking in from the outside, we were just a family dealing with a difficult situation stemming from the birth of a special needs child. Inside our family though, the dynamics of what was happening were so much more dramatic. By embracing Alyssa as God's gift to us, rather than trying to fix her, He was able to work through her to touch not only our lives, but the lives of so many people with which Alyssa brought us into contact. Without ever saying a word, Alyssa brought me and my son to salvation. She brought our whole family unit closer together and closer to God. She touched a number of doctors, nurses, therapists and administrators that worked with her.

I came out of the experience stronger as a person and as a Christian, with a clearer sense of what my priorities in life ought to be. Where my career once topped the list, now the top slot belongs to God. I place my priorities in order now as God, family, country (job). It doesn't mean that I place less importance on my work, but I will no longer base decisions on that as the highest priority. My experience in dealing with Alyssa's condition and subsequent death taught me that life is too fleeting to be wasted on things that aren't important. Ultimately, if I'm not working for God while I'm on this earth, my work means nothing. My eternal life is vastly more important than my temporary existence here.

I view everything through a different lens now, and it changes how I approach situations and how I deal with others. I don't worry now over things. I have learned to just turn them over to God and let Him sort them out according to His will for my life. As much as I love my career, I realized that the Army will continue on unchanged without me, while my family will not. That realization places family considerations as a filter for any career decisions.

Ultimately through Alyssa, I learned to live life each day to its fullest because you never know when it will be your last. By taking this approach with Alyssa, we were able to ensure we had no regrets when she died. I live each day now doing my best to please God, so that when it is my turn to be accountable, I won't have any regrets over the way I lived my life either.

Chapter 6

Ask What, Not Why

One of the first things we do when adversity strikes is to ask the question, "Why?" Why did this happen? Why me? Why us? Why do I have to go through this? It is natural in our human nature to ask these questions, but asking why usually doesn't yield any answers. It seems to merely put us in a downward spiral of negativity. While "Why?" may be the natural first question to ask, we must quickly move past that, or we risk getting stuck in a cycle of negative thinking and negative action.

Focusing on asking why causes us to do four things that pull us away from our relationship with God. First, we take our eyes off God and focus on ourselves. Second, we act as if we are better than everyone else and are somehow above having to deal with such situations. Third, we forget who is really in control. And lastly, we allow anger and doubt to cloud our thinking. All of these things work against our ability to see God's work in the situation at hand and to understand the purpose behind it. A better question to ask is, "What?"

When we ask "why," we immediately look down. This causes us to take our eyes off God and to focus inward on ourselves. We hang our head and start to feel self-pity. By doing this, we are focused on our wants, our desires, and our feelings. In focusing inward, we can completely miss the bigger picture of what is going on around us.

When we look down rather than up, we lose sight of the one who is always there for us no matter how bad the situation gets. Instead we retreat inward and feel as if it's us against the world. More importantly, once we take our eyes off God, we open up an opportunity for the devil to take advantage of the situation and attack us.

If my husband and I had allowed ourselves to get stuck in asking why about our situation, we would have never been able to move forward and do the things we needed to do for our daughter. Instead of focusing on ourselves, we chose to focus on her, and that allowed us to watch God work in her and through her. We were able to see that she truly was special, not just because of her anomalies, but because of the purpose God had for her life. We realized we had to be special parents to help her fulfill that purpose, whatever it was.

When we ask "why," we act as if we are better than everyone else and are somehow above having to deal with such situations. In questioning why something has happened to us, we show our prideful self in thinking that we are somehow special. Does that mean that you wish the tribulation would happen to someone else? If so, that's not a very Christian thought either.

The simple fact of the matter is that as much as we would like no adverse things to happen, they do. At some point in our lives, everyone had to deal with some adversity, with some situations certainly being more negative than others. It is the very nature of the sinful world we live in, the one we created with that first sin in the Garden of Eden.

There are a lot of parents out there who have special needs children born to them, so we didn't feel as if an unfair burden was being placed on us. In fact, we never ever viewed Alyssa as a burden. From the very beginning we accepted that she was the child God intended us to have. We never felt as if we were somehow above having to deal with the situation. She was our special gift, and we would learn as much, if not more, from her, as she would learn from us.

When we ask "why," we forget who is really in control. We feel as if we have lost control of a situation, when in fact, we don't really control anything. Any feeling that we have control over things that happen is really an illusion and denies the existence of our Creator who controls everything.

As we watched Alyssa in the Neonatal Intensive Care Unit, we knew we weren't in control of the situation, but we also knew that even with as much knowledge as the doctors had, they weren't in control either. When they would rely on their textbook answers for Alyssa's case, God would surprise them. Each time they didn't expect her to respond well to a procedure, she would bounce back quicker than anticipated. They didn't think she would survive three weeks, yet she lived more than three years. Each time they said she wouldn't be able to do something, she would turn around and do it. God had complete control of the situation.

And lastly, by asking "why," we allow anger and doubt to cloud our thinking. The simple act of questioning plants the seeds that allow doubt to spring up, and from that, anger can grow. When we ask why, we question God's divine plan. We turn our back on our faithfulness to God, and instead of trusting Him, we question the purpose, the plan, and His will.

Often in times of adversity, people question how a loving God can allow such bad things to happen. The sin in this world was created by man. God gave us free will, and not everyone uses that free will in a positive way. We choose the path we follow. Either we follow God, or we follow what's in the world.

No matter how tempting it might be, the one thing we should never question is the fact that there is a purpose to everything. When God allows man to do negative things, he can still use the situation to bring about good, but we have to maintain our steadfast trust in Him. Never lose sight of the fact that no matter how bad things are, God is in control. We must trust that His will shall be done.

Instead of asking "Why?" when faced with adversity, a better question to ask might be "What?". Lord, what is your purpose for what I am enduring? What am I to learn from this experience? What is it that I should change in my life? What can I do to help others in this situation? By asking these types of questions, we keep our focus where it needs to be, upward and outward.

With a focus on God during the difficult times, we remain open to watching Him work in our lives. We can see how He directs events and be receptive to His will for us in the situation. We are open to His molding and shaping of our lives. When we get stuck in the question of "Why?," there is so much that we can miss out on, potentially even missing the whole purpose of the situation.

I still don't claim to know the purpose behind why Alyssa was born the way she was. I can try to guess with my limited knowledge, but I would probably be wrong or at least incomplete in my assessment. Someday it will be revealed to me. I do know that by focusing on "what" instead of "why," we remained open to what God's will was in the situation.

Keeping an open mind allowed us to marvel at how God worked through Alyssa, a small child who would never utter a word, who would be viewed and discounted by the world as broken, and who would change our lives forever. We were open to Him working through her on us, and through us on others. Our focus allowed us to see when the Lord brought others across our path, either for our benefit or theirs. I am still amazed when I think about it.

By asking "what" instead of "why," we were able to see the blessings in our situation instead of viewing it as a burden. We were able to enjoy our time with our daughter instead of being distressed and angry.

By focusing outward, we were able to impact others and provide hope to them instead of feeling hopeless ourselves. Without a doubt, it was surely a difficult situation, but God was able to use it for so much good, both in our lives and in the lives of others.

Ultimately, I remain convinced that if we had not taken the approach we did, Alyssa would not have lived as long. Our constant love and support buoyed her fighting spirit. She fought because she knew we were fighting for her. Our positive approach helped to create positive outcomes. Our belief in the impossible made it possible. If we had not been able to see the blessings God was giving us, I do not believe he would have continued to bless us with the opportunity to know and love our special little girl.

Chapter 7

Using Our Faith to Lift Up Others

Finally, be ye all of one mind, having compassion one of another, love as brethren, be pitiful, be courteous: Not rendering evil for evil, or railing for railing: but contrariwise blessing; knowing that ye are thereunto called, that ye should inherit a blessing..
1 Peter 3: 8-9

When mired in adversity, we tend to think just of ourselves, focusing mostly on trying to navigate through whatever situation confronts us. However, sometimes the adversity we face isn't about us. Sometimes it is about others whose paths we cross when dealing with a situation. Through adversity, we have opportunities to impact the lives of others both during and after our times of crisis. If we focus inward, we can miss those opportunities, which usually provide more of a blessing to us than those we sought to bless.

The way we handle adversity can be one of the best examples of Christianity to others. Demonstrations of faith during difficult times are living testaments to our beliefs, for those are times when beliefs can waiver. Many people talk about their beliefs during times of peace and tranquility, yet seem to forget everything they have espoused in the past when the storms of life descend. It is easy to talk the talk, but can be very difficult to walk the walk.

I was keenly aware of this fact as I navigated the grief I felt over Alyssa's death. As a baby Christian, having been saved just about 18 months prior, I felt many of those around me were watching to see how I handled the situation, both Christians and non-believers. In one respect, that added pressure to an already difficult situation, but at the same time, it provided me a focus and made me dig really deep into my beliefs. I couldn't just say that I knew Alyssa was in Heaven and I would see her again someday, I had to truly believe it with every fiber of my being, lest I be a hypocrite. My actions had to match and demonstrate my beliefs. I know I didn't always get it right because I'm human, and it was a struggle to deal positively with my grief. But I know I got right more times than not, and the more I dealt with the tug between faith and frailty, the stronger my faith became.

That was not the case with my husband. We seemed to process our grief differently. I went through what typically are presented as the most well-known stages of grief as defined by Elizabeth Kubler-Ross in her book "On Death and Dying" – denial, anger, bargaining, depression, and acceptance. I went through the first two stages very quickly on the first day and almost completely skipped over the bargaining stage because I knew what had happened wasn't reversible. The very limited amount of bargaining I did centered mainly around ensuring the continued safety of my remaining two children. The stage that posed the greatest challenge for me was depression. Having given birth to Aidan just six months prior to Alyssa's death, I was already struggling with postpartum depression, which I had also experienced after my first two pregnancies. The grief from Alyssa's death compounded the problem.

My husband, on the other hand, went straight to the angry stage and stayed there for a very long time. The anger permeated every aspect of his life and began to poison it. He began to act in ways that were not Christian-like at all, and the kids and I took the full brunt of his anger most of the time. It eventually tore the fabric of our marriage apart because he refused to seek help.

I can remember distinct moments during Alyssa's life when dealing with her challenges made us cross paths with others who reached out and were a blessing to us. A nurse who provided encouragement during tough medical times. A woman who came up to me in the waiting room one time and prayed with me over Alyssa.

My faith-based approach to parenting Alyssa also allowed me to reach out to others because I was open to the promptings the Lord gave me. Those opportunities allowed me to use my own adversity to provide a message or a blessing to others. I reached out to provide support to other parents whose children just arrived in the Neonatal Intensive Care Unit after we had been there for a while. I gave a presentation to a group of hospital interns to provide the perspective of a parent of a special needs child and advised them not to define their patients by their diagnosis. So many people commented to us that the positive way in which we approached our parenting challenges was an inspiration to them. Even after hearing that many times, I didn't develop a true appreciation for what that meant until much later.

In addition to being able to use your faith to boost others during the actual times of adversity, we can also use the perspective, strength and resilience gained after enduring traumatic events and reaching the other side to help others.

Crises and tragedies can mold us and shape us and perhaps provide newfound perspective on life, but we shouldn't allow them to define us. If we allow an event to define us, the event is the focus and remains such, to the point where it can become a crutch used throughout life. A better avenue is to let our strength of character define us both during and after adversity. It is that strength of character, coupled with faith, which can have a profound effect on others if you are open to the Lord's promptings to engage.

I used to be surprised when I felt compelled to say something to someone, only to hear them tell me, "You don't know how much I needed to hear that."

I'm not surprised anymore. I know that when I listen to the Lord's whispers about what to say, or when I go where he tells me to go, I find that I have incredible opportunities to touch the lives of others. Those opportunities also bring me incredible blessings and satisfaction and further strengthen my faith.

I experienced this not too long ago when we moved and were in the process of trying to find a new church. We had attended a church several times and were really feeling comfortable with the thought of making that our church. The Sunday service followed a format of group worship first and then breaking out into groups called "connect" groups for continued reflection and study. The connect groups were organized by age and/or stages of life and topical breakdowns. I had tried one connect group the first week but found that it didn't fit my needs. The second week I was going to try a different group centered around learning about the church and its beliefs and programs.

When I showed up for the group, the leader remarked that it was more of a class and probably below the level I was looking for. He suggested I visit the group next door. Feeling that the Lord was leading me somewhere special, I followed. As the group introduced themselves and asked for prayer requests, there wasn't anything particularly remarkable until one woman spoke. She explained that she had a praise for her son finishing physical therapy and beginning to walk but then stated that her son had been diagnosed as mildly autistic and they were trying to figure out just what that would mean for him and his progress. She also stated that she had just found out she was pregnant again, and asked for prayers for a healthy child. As she told her story, my heart ached for her, but I knew why I had been sent to that group that day. After the group, I approached her and told her that I had walked in her shoes and knew what she was going through. I gave her all of my contact information and told her to call if she ever needed to talk or vent or cry. Another woman approached us as we talked and said she had heard our conversation and that she was writing a book about loss. She asked if I would be willing to be interviewed as part of her book. That morning provided additional validation for my walk of faith and willingness to go where the Lord led me. Just because I listened to the whispers in my heart, I was able to touch two people that day.

Every day we have the opportunity to touch others in unique and special ways if only we are open to the possibility. Adversity provides us unique opportunities for interaction with others hungry for a message of hope. By focusing outward instead of inward, we'll see the opportunities presented to us. If we focus inward, we miss the chance to impact the lives of others. It is hard work sometimes to look for the blessings in times of adversity, but they are there in abundance. Just hold onto your faith and look up not down. Ask what, not why, and you'll come out of the experience stronger for having gone through it and better equipped to help others navigate the rocky road.

CONCLUSION

Since my daughter's death, I have had plenty of other trying times in my life, and I am sure there are plenty more to come. Because of my experiences though, I face each trial with a new perspective.

My newfound willingness to let go has enriched my life immeasurably. By not trying to control things, I am enjoying the ride more because there are surprises around every corner. I don't try to anticipate the twists and turns; I just go with the flow.

I know the Lord has me in the palm of his hand and will provide what I need when I need it. I know that it's not all about me, so I look for those opportunities to touch others. In turn, I am touched as well.

And the mission continues…

www.ingramcontent.com/pod-product-compliance
Ingram Content Group UK Ltd.
Pitfield, Milton Keynes, MK11 3LW, UK
UKHW041944230426
12048UKWH00008B/122